Through the Hedges

Elias Estrada

BookLeaf Publishing

India | USA | UK

Presentation by *BookLeaf Publishing*

Web: www.bookleafpub.com

E-mail: info@bookleafpub.com

ISBN: 9789360943691

First edition 2024

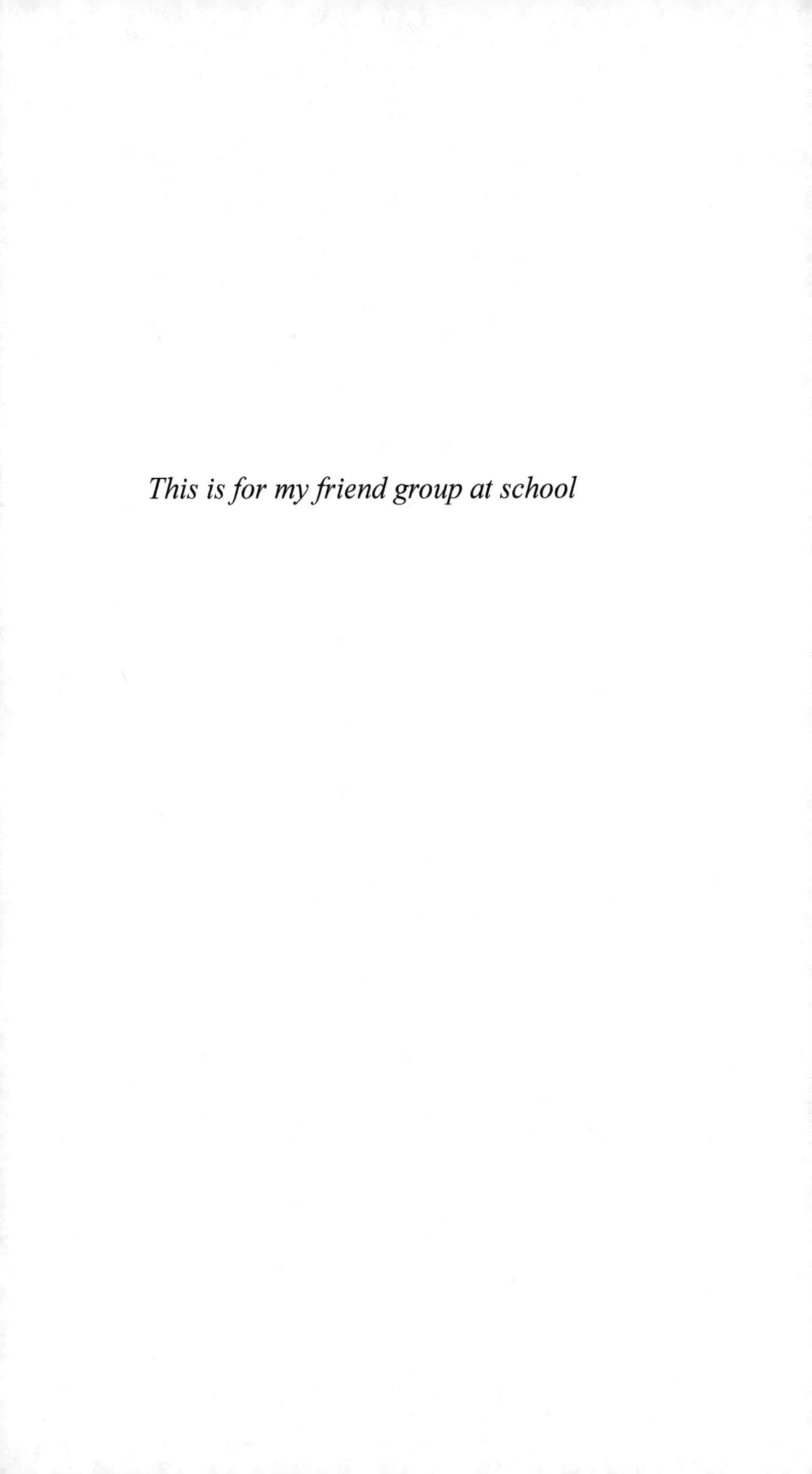

This is for my friend group at school

Mystery Guy (a simile poem)

You're as smart as an elephant,
as cocky as a chick
You're as glorious as an ant
crawling on a stick
Your smile is whiter than the stars in the sky
oh how I wonder who you are, mystery guy.

A Boy Who Was Six

a boy who was six
went out to pick sticks
for his mom and dad

he came out from the yard
breathing real hard
and made his parents glad

he looked at his mom
and said "hey, I picked sticks"
his mom looked and smiled
and then gave him a kiss

his dad saw what happened
and said "good job champ!
I should sign you up for stick-picking camp!"

Red Rocket

Red rocket in the sky
Red rocket up so high
Red rocket show your flare
Shine your fire everywhere
Go up high and reach the stars
Red Rocket go so far
Go to planets, go to suns
Just come back when you're done.

Insects

In the leaves
Not inside
Sits an insect
Ending its hide
Coming out
To see the sky
So he can watch the sun set and rise.

Superdog

5

the perfect dog
my pup Pinky
taking a nap in the sun
or sleeping with me
chewing on a sock
or eating her treats
cute little Pinky
was made just for me

Lunch with my Friend Group

like a circus full of clowns
who make you laugh so good
You'll stop with the frowns
and smile like you should
the Rose gets reading
the Falcon laughs a lot
the rest keep eating
and make jokes to keep the laughs hot.

A Very Big Forest

In a very big forest
stood a very big rock
with very big moss
that stank of gym socks
and that very big smell
caused a very big guy
who just walked by
to almost cry
he squeezed his big nose
and said in a big voice
"I hate this rock
take it down, boys!"
then a very big crane
with a big wrecking ball
slammed into the rock
but didn't destroy it all
the big guy got angry
and took his big hands
he picked up the rock
and crushed it into sand
but the moss fell and no one would see
it stayed there forever
as lonely as can be

The Colored Camel

Once there was a camel
with more than 2 humps
he had all kinds of colored bumps-
ones that were dotted,
spotted, and ziggy
humps so bright
they could make a man jiggy
his name was Humphidityhumphix
how many humps did he have?
26,478,912,326

A Tree's Point Of View

Hi I'm a tree
and I'm stuck in the ground
I'm for hiding children
waiting to be found
I'm made for climbing
I'm made for homes
I'm made for the little homeless gnomes
Im producing oxygen
for life itself
what an honor
to get trash dumped on myself.

Cake pops

a hard outer shell
to crunch when hungry
with some cake frosting filling
to stuff your tummy
the flavors and textures
taste so good
cake pops are iconic
for everyone's childhood

Cutie My Cute Kitty

A cat so fat
the cover cant cover
the one thing needed in life
and I love her
a cat so lazy
she rolls to her food
a cat so grumpy
she's always in a mood

When I Grow Up

When I'm old I'll shove my face full of sweets
When I'm old I'll drop some sick beats
When I'm old I'll watch TV while eating Lays
When I'm old I'll visit Mom for days
When I'm old I'll hang out with my friends
and call my siblings until the end

Sick

A clogged-up nose,
so sniffing is out.
A mask to protect you
from getting your sickness about.
A hurt stomach,
a big migraine.
Lots of drowsiness,
and lots of pain.
Lots of gross medicine
that tastes really bad.
It's a sickness that makes you feel very sad.

New stuff

you've used your allowance
and bought something new
it could be something to wear
or something to do
something to drink
or something to eat
but whatever it is
it's real neat

Poetry

Placing
One line
Every rhyme
To be just fine
Reading it?
Your job and mine.

Guilt

You've lied to your mom,
your friend, or your dad
And when they find out
they'll be really mad
but until then
the guilt comes in
and you lose to guilt
because guilt always wins
they found out
and they got mad
at what you've done
thinking it was fun
was actually really bad

A Little Haiku

a little haiku
made its way in a big book
funny how things work

a little haiku
was written by an author
in a poem book

a little haiku
it has big things and small things
it made it so far

School Metaphor

School is sunshine that isn't bright
School is a circus that has no clowns
School is a sea that has no water
School is a smile that's called a frown
School can be boring
but also fun
especially the last day
when you're done

About The Author

just a kid
in a world of adults
with my words to help
stuff like insults
my pets, so cute
my friend, so cool
my mom, so clear
you could call her a pool
my life, so boring
with little fun things
I pass the boredom
with writings

Things I Can Cram In (that I like)

Taco Tuesday
Happy people
Ideas that make me feel mischievous
Nothing that annoys me
Getting money
Someone who I outwit

Through the hedges

Through the hedges
a hedgehog trots
walking to the berry bush
its favorite spot
joined by her friends
a dog and a cat
one who is biting a sock
and the other who is fat
they munch on berries
and laugh all day long
not a care in the world
while they eat along
such a beautiful moment
a sight to see
the three friends talking
with mouths full of berry